The Eight Hour Day
By Tom Mann

What a Compulsory 8 Hour Working Day
Means to the Workers

and

The Workers' Demand

1886 & 1892

With an introduction by Terry McCarthy

Reprint pamphlet No 1. The Eight Hour Day. Tom Mann
This edition, with introduction by Terry McCarthy, published 2008
Copyright © Terry McCarthy 2008
All rights reserved

LHM *Labour History Movement*

Other publications about the Labour movement, including original pamphlet reprints and Trade Union emblems are available.

Cover Illustration: Gas Workers' Union Emblem

ISBN 978-0-9556923-1-4

Contents

Introduction		page 5
Tract One.	What a Compulsory 8 Hour Working Day Means to the Workers	page 9
Tract Two.	The Workers' Demand	page 25
Further Reading		page 50
Supplementary Note	Walter Southgate	page 51

Introduction

Tom Mann was born in Coventry in 1856. He left school at the age of nine to begin work as a quarry worker, later taking up an engineering apprenticeship. His views were not determined simply by political theory - it was from practical experience gained over many years while working on every continent. Mann's religious belief was as strong as his politics, and he supported non-conformist organisations like the Salvation Army. Mann soon turned to socialism.

He moved to London in 1877 and by 1881 was a member of the Engineers Union ASE. His first involvement in a strike came in 1884. Mann then published his pamphlet on the eight-hour day. Mann helped organise the Match Workers' strike of 1888 and he began producing a Socialist journal, the 'Labour Elector'. The Gas Workers' successful strike in 1889 for the eight- hour day was possibly the most political of all of the new union strikes that year. The Gas Workers' leader Will Thorne was ably assisted by Ben Tillett, Tom Mann, John Burns, Harry Hobbit, Harry Quelch and Herbert Burrows: a formidable team.

The skilled workers unions had been asking for the eight-hour day for decades, in fact, one of the first aims of the Trades Union Congress, formed in 1868, was to campaign for the eight-hour day; the difference being that once the so-called unskilled unions were formed, as in the case of the gas workers, they *demanded* the eight-hour day which they achieved through industrial action. This demonstrated the difference between the liberal TUC and the Socialist inspired New Union movement. Mann not only articulated the logic of the eight-hour day through his great oratory delivered throughout length and breadth of Britain, he wrote 'What a compulsory 8 hour working day means to the Workers' in 1886. The pamphlet was written three years before the successful strike for the eight hour day by gas workers in Beckton, East London.

At the time of writing this pamphlet the eight-hour day seemed unrealisable to the then leaders of the Trade union movement. Interestingly, in the tract Mann mentions the bad conditions in the Bryant and May Match factory whose workers were to play such a crucial role in the formation on the New Union movement. Mann was one of the leaders of the 1889 Dock Strike and was elected President of the Dock Wharf Riverside and General Labourers Union. Along with Quelch and Tom McCarthy he acted as mediator with the all-important South London Dockers who were often alienated by Tillet's dictatorial style. Mann tried unsuccessfully to form a Super Union from the legions of unions that were formed in 1889 -1890 as a way to combat the coming power of the Multinationals. Unfortunately sectarian interests prevailed, weakening the Labour movement in the process.

In 1892, three years after the winning of the eight-hour day by the gas workers, and the formation of the New Union movement, Mann wrote 'The Workers' Demand The Eight Hour Day'. The sceptics within the TUC and skilled workers unions were now silent: the dream of the eight-hour day now seemed realisable.

In 1895, Tom Mann, by now national figure, became a founder-member of the Independent Labour Party. Not everybody agreed with Tom Mann's views. He had many enemies on the right of the Labour

Introduction

movement and was defeated in the ASE election where he stood for the post of Secretary. However, in 1896 he did become President of the International Transport Workers' Federation which he had helped to create. In 1898, along with Tom Chambers, he helped launch the Workers' Union, a small but militant organisation.

Mann now started his International campaign, forming unions and preaching international solidarity and unity. This did not go down well with the authorities and he was deported from a number of European countries on the grounds of sedition. He first began agitating in New Zealand before moving onto Australia and organising for the Australian Labour Party. He had his first taste of imprisonment in Australia, in 1906, the charge: again, sedition. This did little to dampen Mann's spirit – he moved to South Africa, where continued his activities organising and agitating.

Returning to the UK in 1910, Mann noted that many of the firebrands of the 1880's had become reformist. He argued that socialism could not be achieved without the trade unions playing a major role. It was during this period that Tom Mann was reunited with his old comrade from America 'Big' Bill Haywood (Mann had assisted Haywood's IWW movement whilst in America). They had long discussions on the way forward for the international labour movement.

Mann then founded the syndicalist education league. It's a misassumption to conclude that the English syndicalist movement was on a par with that in France in terms of ideology. Mann fully understood the loathing of political theory and ideology amongst organised labour: his was a very British syndicalism.

Despite their political and personal differences, Ben Tillett invited Mann to become an organiser in the 1911 Liverpool transport strike. Tom Mann raced to the assistance of James Larkin, James Connolly and the Dublin strikers in 1913 -14, and again during this dispute linked up with comrade Bill Haywood. The TUC was totally opposed to Larkin and the strike and withdrew its support leading to the defeat of the strike.

Mann was totally opposed to the First World War and was prosecuted for sedition. In 1917 he joined the British Socialist Party, and in that same year, was a firm supporter of the Bolshevik revolution. In 1919, despite his earlier defeat over 20 years previously, he became the secretary of the Amalgamated Society of Engineers, retiring in 1921. He was chairman of the rank and file National Minority movement which built a strong base in all sections of the trade union movement much to the annoyance of the TUC, and he was a founder member of the Communist Party in 1920.

He tried unsuccessfully to enlist in the International Brigade but was denied because of his age, although he raised funds and spoke on many occasions both in the UK and in Spain. He also worked with Wal Hannington and the unemployed workers movement.

At the age of 75 he was indicted for sedition in Belfast after making inflammatory speeches. Famously, the judge said to him before sentencing: "someone your age should know better". To which Tom Mann replied: "Sir, the longer I live and the more I see here and around the world I know my course is right".

He died a poor man, at least in financial terms, in Leeds in 1941, but rich in terms of his legacy to the Labour and Trade Union movement.

Terry McCarthy

What a Compulsory 8 Hour Working Day Means to the Workers

Tom Mann, 1886

Oh Slaves of these laborious years,
    Oh Freemen of the years to be:
Shake off your blind and foolish fears,
    And hail the Truth that makes you free.

The appalling amount of distress that exists in every town in Britain must arrest the attention of all duty loving men and women. No one who sees the effects of want and the fear of want can passively behold the dire poverty of a large section of the workers. Rather will he probe and probe until he finds the cause of the disease. Socialists *have* probed and they find the disease of want to be spread by the profit-making system upon which all industry and society itself is based. They know that five or six centuries ago, without machinery, Englishmen obtained for their work sufficient to keen them in vigorous health and that they were not subject to periodical trade depressions; and when they further reflect upon the fact that the working day then consisted of no more than eight hours, no wonder that socialists are discontented with the present state of affairs, and that they resolve to use every means in their power to replace the present discord, misery, and anarchy, with harmony, happiness, and order.

The effect of our so-called labour-saving machinery (used really by its owners to save *wages* and not *labour*) is to cause continual distress amongst the workers by mercilessly throwing them out of employment without any compensation. It may then take a man often months, sometimes years, to find an occupation of any kind and when found it is at a price much below that he was in receipt of before the machine disturbed him. Yet the machine has increased the ease and rapidity of wealth-production. This increase of wealth is of course enriching *someone* - a class of which many perform but little really useful work while the bulk of them serve no function useful in any way to the community. Look, again, at the effect of increased scientific knowledge. By a better knowledge of chemistry and metallurgy tons of metal are now extracted from the ore with the labour of fewer men than must formerly have been employed to produce one hundredweight. What I am concerned about is, that in spite of our advanced methods of producing wealth, the workers as a class get only a subsistence wage, whilst an increasing number of them cannot get the barest necessaries of life.

Optimist politicians are unwilling to admit that this is so. Anxious to make out a good case for the present basis of society, they ignore the plainest of facts, so in confirmation of my contention I will quote from one or two non-socialists. Professor Thorold Rogers, the present MP for Bermondsey, says on pages 185-6 of 'Six Centuries of Work and Wages', written in 1884:

> 'It may be well the case, and there is every reason to fear it is the case, that there is collected a population in our great towns which equals in extent the whole of those who lived

in England and Wales six centuries ago; but whose condition is more destitute, whose homes are more squalid, whose means are more uncertain, whose prospects are more hopeless than those of the poorest serfs of the Middle Ages and the meanest drudges of the mediaeval cities. The arm of the law is strong enough to keep them under, and society has no reason to fear their despair; but I refuse to accept the superficial answer that a man is an admirer of the good old times because he insists that the vaunts of civilisation should be examined along with, and not apart from its failures. It is not possible to give the solution of one problem, the growth of opulence, and to refuse all attention to the other problem, the growth of penury.'

Joseph Cowen MP speaking at a Mechanics' Institute at Newcastle, alluded to the labouring section as 'a hybrid class doomed to eat the bread of penury and drink the cup of misery. Precarious labour provided them with subsistence for the day, but the slightest interruption threw them destitute. A week of broken weather brought thousands of these industrial nomads to the brink of starvation. An inscrutable influence seemed to sink them as it elevated those around and above them. Society, ashamed and despairing, swept them, like refuse, into dismal receptacles, where seething in their wretchedness, they constituted at once our weakness and reproach. How to sweeten these receptacles and help their forlorn occupants to help themselves was the problem of the hour. *If society did not settle it, it would in time settle society.* '

To this socialists answer that there is no permanent way of sweetening the lives of the class referred to except by the complete annihilation of the profit-mongers as a class, by forcing them all into the ranks of the *useful* workers. This will be apparent when it is realised that under the present system we are working to supply profits to profit-mongers instead of working to supply the legitimate requirements of the entire community, and when it is borne in mind that shareholders and employers are contented with nothing less than the *highest* possible profits, it will also be seen that on the other hand we (the workers) can have nothing more than the *lowest* possible wages. To establish society on a proper basis is therefore the work of every right-minded man or woman.

Demagogues have been at work - with good intentions perhaps - but they have misled the workers from the true cause of their troubles. Among the blind leaders of the blind may be mentioned the Malthusians, the Teetotallers, the Financial Reformers, and well-intentioned Radicals. The first mentioned have taught that there are too many people in the country, and that the only way of bettering our condition is by curtailing the population, and this in face of the fact that every year wealth in this country is increasing much faster than population. The Temperance advocates hammer away at the blessings of sobriety as though drunkenness was the cause of poverty, when the fact is the other way about. Well nigh as fast as they surround an old toper with influences that prevent his drinking tastes being gratified, another fills up the hole out of which he was lifted. It is a useless expenditure of energy to be continually preaching temperance and thrift. Let all be blest with leisure, food and healthy enjoyments, as they might be if the economic basis of society was as it should be, and then these matters will all right themselves. The only reason people spend time upon these panaceas is because they fail to understand the law of wages, which is that all above a bare subsistence wage shall go to profit mongers as profit. The only way out is to *destroy the profit mongers*.

The same argument applies to the financial reformer. All sensible persons are of course agreed that the country should be governed as economically as is consistent with efficiency, as also all are agreed that we should live soberly. But the reformer fails to see that if we curtail taxation to its lowest possible minimum, reduce it if you will 90 per cent, not one farthing of it would be saved to the workers. The Iron Law would still be in force which says, 'So much as will keep life in you *and no more* shall go to you, 0 ye workers, so long as the profit making system remains.'

These economic questions cannot be understood in a sufficiently clear manner by the mass of the workers while they are absorbed twelve, fourteen, sixteen, and even more hours a day while in work, and when out of work are walking about with the pangs of hunger eating out their vitals, and the blackness of despair staring them in the face at every turn. Now suppose those of us who can see these things in something like their grim reality, decide that come what may, we at least will do our part towards obtaining remunerative employment for all, and at the same time sufficient leisure that all may have a little breathing time after their work, what course can we take? To this I reply, there is one way by which it can be done, viz, by at once concentrating our efforts towards the establishing of an eight hours working day.

Let us examine a few figures in order to see clearly how this would affect us. We have something like 7,000,000 adult workers in the British Isles, working nominally under the nine hours system, leaving overtime out of consideration for the moment. Let us see how many more hands would be put in employment if we struck off one hour per day from those in work. It is roughly estimated that of the above mentioned workers there are about 900,000 now out of work, representing a total population of 3 and a half or 4 millions of men, women, and children who cannot get the barest necessaries of life. Now strike off one hour per day from the 6,000,000 in work. The result would be an immediate demand for 750,000 additional workers to keep up production at its present rate, and remembering that these 750,000 would immediately begin to buy more food, clothing, and general comforts, this of course would give an impetus to trade, and so add greatly to the comfort of the entire community for a year or two. These advantages, however, would soon be swallowed up by fresh displacements of labour due to more efficient machinery and advancing scientific knowledge; but, during the year or two that it gave relief, see how immensely it would add to the leisure and therefore to the general intelligence of the workers. And increased intelligence means more active discontent with our conditions of life, and in due course a hastening of the overthrow of the present capitalistic domination.

I am fully aware that there are some who claim to have a knowledge of the workers who contend that the very success of an Eight Hours Movement would simply mean a perpetuation of the present wretched system, as the people would become more contented if the conditions of life were made more tolerable. This I hold to be the very reverse of truth. As a workman who has worked from early boyhood on the farm, down the mine, and in the engineer's shop, I repudiate such a slanderous statement. What means the continually increasing restlessness of late years of those workmen who are now, *relatively* to their former position, in a passable state of comfort? I contend that it is in large part due to the additional leisure obtained under the nine hours system, though most of its advantages have now been swallowed up by more rapid machinery and the cursed system of overtime we still tolerate. I ask myself what has been my guide in the formation of my opinions on social and political subjects, and, risking being charged with egotism, I reply that I have ever endeavoured to get correct views upon these and other subjects by fashioning my ideas upon the best models I could find, and the more leisure I had the better my opportunity for finding good models. I can understand a middle-class man holding this - to me - absurd theory. I can also understand some workmen reflecting the opinions of these theory-loving, poverty-accentuating blockheads merely because they are middle-class. But I cannot understand a workman who through youth and early manhood has been battling against long hours in order that he might attend the institute, listen to the lectures, and read the works of able men and by these means has succeeded in having a mind worth owning - I say I cannot understand such an one hindering rather than helping in a shorter hours movement. He practically says by such conduct that the leisure he used so well as to become a man thereby, others will use so ill that they will continue fools. But men generally love what is best for all, and are prepared to do their part towards carrying it out so soon as they understand clearly what course they should take. Let those of us who see (or think we see) further than the average man, do all in our power towards enabling him to see as clearly as we do, and then, unless I am incapable of reading aright the lesson of life, he too will become in his turn an earnest and an energetic worker for the elevation of his class. I must apologise to some readers who may think that none of this reasoning is necessary. I emphasise it because I know there exist philosophers who strain at gnats and swallow camels, who talk of ameliorating human suffering, but hang back instead of assisting a movement the success of which must for a dead certainty largely ameliorate the pangs of the hungry men, women, and children who are now in the throes of despair.

Another section raise the objection that however desirable it may be to curtail the hours of labour, remembering the severe competition of other countries it is simply impossible either to raise wages or shorten hours unless a similar movement takes place on the continent. I will endeavour to answer this first by showing that the English workers produce more per man than any of the continental nations, and second, by showing that with regard to our staple industries foreign competition is a bogie used by the employer to frighten the workers into accepting harder terms in order that their master may make a greater profit. It may be of some service to point out the relative wealth per annum produced by the useful workers of this and other countries. I am assuming that the reader is clear concerning the source of wealth, that there is no other source than useful labour, so that, having sufficient raw material for workers to exercise their ingenuity upon, it will be seen that the more workers, the more the aggregate wealth, as in all ages men have been able to produce by their labour more than they and their families required for ordinary consumption. Quoting from Mulhall's 'Statistics', we find that Britain with a population of 36 millions produces wealth to the amount of £1,247,000,000 per annum; France with 37 and a half millions of people produces annually £965,000,000 (or with a million and a half more people about three-quarters the amount the English make), Germany, population 45 millions, wealth per annum, £850,000,000; (or two thirds only of our amount); Russia with 80 millions of people, creates per annum only £760,000,000, Austria, 38 millions population, only £602,000,000 per annum; and similarly with the smaller nations. These figures will serve to show that our method of producing wealth is a more effective one than that in vogue on the continent, as although they generally work longer hours per day than the English yet the result of their year's work compares unfavourably with ours. The important lesson to be learnt here is this that it is not the amount paid as wages that decides whether or not one country can compete successfully with another; or rather, it is not the countries where wages are low that compete most successfully with this country. This will be seen when it is realised that severest competitor we have to-day is America, a country that pays at least 25 per cent higher wages than are paid in this country.

This of itself should be sufficient to encourage those timorous mortals who are always attributing our exhausting toil to the competition of the long hours of the continent. The time may arrive when, with an equally advanced method of production, low paid labour will produce wealth as effectively as better paid labour, but that time has not yet come. By way of proving this let me here instance the iron shipbuilding industry. Many have been the disputes between employers and employed in this industry during the past two or three years, the employers continually urging that the continental shipbuilders are getting all the trade, or at any rate will do so, unless our workmen submit to reductions in wages and longer hours. This argument was advanced repeatedly during the year 1885, so in order to thoroughly test the matter a delegation of workers was despatched to the continent to bring back precise information upon the subject. They found that Germany was our chief competitor in iron shipbuilding, and that during the year 1885 that country produced 22,326 tons of shipping. But in this country one firm on the Clyde during the same period turned out 40,000 tons. France produced 10,000 tons, and Russia 7,867 tons - total for the two countries 17,867 tons. But the river Tyne alone launched no less than 102,998 tons. The Belgium output was 5,312 tons, that of Holland 2,651 tons, of Denmark 3,515 tons. To sum up, the whole of the continental output was a little over 50,000 tons, while that of the English shipyards was 540,282 tons, or nearly eleven times as great as that of all the yards on the continent put together. With facts like these before us is it not high time we demanded that our hours were curtailed so as to give a chance to those who now walk about in enforced idleness, without waiting for the continent to take simultaneous action. The Americans, who pay their mechanics better wages, have had to concede the demands of their workmen for the eight hour working day - not universally, it is true, because a universal demand was not made. Just as their success stimulates us, so our success will stimulate the continental workers, and we shall find that they are as well prepared as we are to deal vigorously with the exploiting classes.

To trade unionists I desire to make a special appeal. How long, *how long* will you be content with the present half-hearted policy of your unions? I readily grant that good work has been done in the past by the unions, but, in heaven's name, what good purpose are they serving now? All of them have large numbers out of employment even when their particular trade is busy. None of the important societies have any policy other than that of endeavouring to keep wages from falling. The true unionist policy of *aggression* seems entirely lost sight of; in fact the unionist of to-day should be of all men the last to be hopelessly apathetic, or supporting a policy that plays directly into the hands of the capitalist exploiter. Do not think I am a non-unionist myself, and therefore denounce unionists. I take my share of the work in the trade union to which I belong, but I candidly confess that unless it shows more vigour in the future than it is showing at the present time (June, 1886) I shall be compelled to take the view - against my will - that to continue to spend time over the ordinary squabble-investigating, do-nothing policy will be an unjustifiable waste of one's energies. I am quite sure there are thousands of others in my state of mind - e.g. all those who concurred with T R Threlfall, the president of the Trades' Union Congress, when, in his presidential address, he told the delegates assembled at Southport that a critical time had arrived in the history of trades unions, and that in the future they must *lead* or *follow*, and that they could not hope to retain advanced men with their present policy. In his magnificent address Mr Threlfall did all a man could do to stir the unionists up to take action in regard to the eight hour working day, but one looks in vain at each and all of our important trade societies to find any action being taken in the matter. It is not enough to say their funds are low. Their funds are not too low to get up an agitation upon this subject. All over the country they have excellent organisations which might be used in the first place as the means for instructing their own members up to the required standard, and then spreading information amongst the non-unionists, skilled and unskilled alike. When the bulk of these understood the pros and cons of the case the combined forces could make a demand for the immediate passing of an Eight Hours Bill, the details of which could be settled by a duly qualified committee.

While this is being done attention should also be made to another important item alluded to by Mr Threlfall viz, the payment of election expenses out of the local or imperial rates and the support of Members of Parliament in a similar manner. When this is done we shall be able to command the services of those whom we believe in because of their merits, irrespective of what the depth of their pocket may be.

The Eight Hour Day

Let me now invite attention to the effects of an Eight Hour Bill upon some of our monopolies. Let us take the railways as a representative concern, using round figures such as will convey a correct idea to the ordinary reader without confusing him. The Blue Books bear out the following statements: - At the present time the annual income of the

British Railways may be put at £70,000,000, of this vast sum one half goes to the shareholders, who do no useful work whatever; one fourth to keep up rolling stock, permanent way etc; and the remaining fourth to the workers, (including managers' and superintendents' salaries).

The man who has not paid attention to railway income and expenditure will denounce this as trash or probably by a stronger term. He will probably say that the figures must be wrong, as railway shareholders get only some 5 per cent on their capital. Exactly, but where nearly all make the mistake is in not making the distinction between percentage on money invested and percentage of income. There are nominally more than £920,000,000 invested in railways in the British Isles, and 5 per cent on this means about five-eighths of the total income, the entire income of 70 millions amounting only to 8 per cent on the investments. Consequently a railway company paying 4 and a half per cent to shareholders actually pays more than half of the total income to these utterly useless individuals, leaving the remainder to go in about equal proportions to rolling stock and permanent way and as wages and salaries to employees. This gives about 18s per week to the 350,000 persons engaged on railways in the British Isles. When we remember that superintendents and managers get very large salaries, we see that those who do the hard work and have the longest hours get much less than 18s.

What a Compulsory 8 Hour Working Day Means to the Workers'

Now that we realise the enormous amount the idle shareholders take, let us see how generously they behave to those in their employ. At Nine Elms are situated the Cleaning sheds of the South Western Railway. Until recently the 'dirty cleaners' at this yard received £1 0s 6d per week. Instructions have been issued from Waterloo to curtail their wages from 20s 6d to 15s at one stroke. On the same line, at Waterloo terminus, the parcels porters commence work at 5.20 in the morning and keep on till 9.45 in the evening with one Sunday off per fortnight, their wages being from 18s to 22s per week.

Now assuming the average day on railways to be 12 hours, what loss would it inflict on the shareholders if a Bill were passed enforcing an eight hours working day? We have seen that the employees get about a quarter of the total income or about £ 17,000,000. To curtail the hours by one third means of course putting one half more men in work than are at present employed. To pay these at a similar rate to those already working would require £8,500,000 or less than one per cent on the nominal value of the shares, so that a company paying 4 and a half per cent now, would, if one half more men were employed still pay 3 and a half per cent to the fleecing shareholders. What arrant nonsense then it is to urge that the company cannot afford to curtail hours.

Let us look now at the conditions of our colliers. Here we have men devoting themselves to underground toil from boyhood to old age, the majority never having the opportunity of paying a visit to the capital, or any other large town, practically kennelled in the earth, tied down with capitalistic chains, '*Spending a sunless life in the unwholesome mines*' for the wretched pittance of about 18s per week. Surely an Eight Hours Bill requires no urging from me on behalf of those who work in and about the mines; when we remember that of the value of coal raised annually in this country (about £66,000,000) one third only goes to the colliers who raise it.

An item worth mentioning also was pointed out by Sir Lyon Playfair in his address before the British Association at Aberdeen in 1885, whilst deploring the fact that the exhaustion of the British coalfields made the coal increasingly difficult to get. It was proved that not only has man's ingenuity conquered these obstacles, but owing to the increased power of steam engines and hand-labour-saving appliances, two men now produce as much as three men did twenty years ago. Yet coal is *dearer* now than it was then!

Thirty years ago eight sailors were required for the management of every 100 tons of shipping. Now, owing to improved machinery, less than half that number suffice. In twenty years the consumption of fuel on our ocean-going steamers has been reduced by one half, chiefly owing to the use of compound engines in place of single ones as formerly. Thus on every hand a greater result is being shown with less labour. And it must be so or else there is no meaning in material progress. But 'less labour' means under our existing system, and must mean so as long as industry is controlled by the idle classes, not 'more leisure' or shorter hours all round, but *less wages*, more unemployed, poverty, famine, and physical and moral degradation.

What then can be more rational than to ease the burden of those in work and the starving stomachs of those who are out, by shortening the working day?

See what is going on in the watch-making industry, a fine example of the effects of machinery. Among the exhibits at last year's Inventions Exhibition was that of the Waltham Watch Co. Some machines were there at work making screws for watches, of which it took 250,000 to make up a pound in weight. These machines were so perfectly made, that at the company's factory in Massachusetts, one boy keeps seven of them going. The best wire to make one pound weight of screws costs ten shillings, but after this wire has been converted into screws by passing through this automatic machine, the screws are worth £350, or seven hundred times the cost of the material. Imagine the number of men here thrown out of employment; the watches in large part being made by girls, and the enormous profits going to the owners of the machinery.

Take another case, that of Bryant and May's match factory in East London. Two years ago this firm was formed into a limited liability company. Their work girls are most miserably paid, getting only some 8s per week, and the company refused to increase their pay when they made a demand a short time since. And yet that company, during the first *six* months of its existence, after paying all working expenses, actually paid over £33,000 to shareholders, who had not done a single stroke of work towards producing it. These girls are working ordinary factory hours, 10 and a half per day. They cannot live in comfort on such a miserable pittance as they are receiving. How many girls are compelled by this sort of thing, to take to the streets?

The above is only typical of what all our large firms are doing. Armstrong, Mitchell and Co, the great engineering firm at Newcastle-on-Tyne, for instance, last year after deducting for working expenses and depreciation of stock, paid to shareholders £162,000.

Whatever improvement may come through more efficient machinery etc, its effect, while owned by, and used for the profit of, the employing class, will be to throw men out of work and swell the already too full pockets of the capitalists. If we do not decide to curtail the hours of labour, what then can we do? Allow things to go from bad to worse? That is what most assuredly will happen, unless we absorb the unemployed into the ranks of the employed by rigidly suppressing overtime, and curtailing the nominal nine hours per day to something less.

The question will be asked by some, 'What about wages if we work an hour a day less, are we to have an hour's less pay?' Most certainly not. Even when the curtailing principle was only partially applied 15 years ago by the trade unionists this did not happen. On the contrary in many instances the workmen were soon able to get a rise in actual wages in addition to the curtailing of hours. The reason we cannot command a better wage now is because the employer can say, 'If you don't like it you may go, others will be glad to take your place,' but, as I think I have shown, if we make eight hours the labour day when the unemployed will be absorbed and the workers will be able in their turn to dictate terms to the employer.

In conclusion I appeal to the workers of Great Britain to join hands over this business and let us make it a success. In a measure of this kind Liberal and Tory, Christian and freethinker, unionist and non-unionist, mechanic and labourer, radical and social-democrat, teetotaller or vegetarian, whatsoever be your creed or sex, unite on common ground and let us fight this battle of the workers with vigour, with energy and determination. Be no longer apathetic. Take pleasure in the performance of your duty as an honest citizen and the result will be a hastening of that glorious time when the domination of a class shall be a matter of history, and when all shall have enough work and none shall have too much.

The Workers' Demand The Eight Hour Day

Tom Mann, 1892

> T hen let us pray that come it may,
> As come it will for a' that,
> That sense and worth o'er a' the earth,
> May bear the gree and a' that.
>
> For a' that and a' that,
> It's coming yet for a' that,
> That man to man, the world o'er,
> Shall brothers be for a 'that.
>
> Burns

The Workers' Demand

The result of much discussion during the past few years, as to the effect likely to follow upon the reduction of the hours of labour, has made it clear that to reduce the working hours in this country to a maximum of 48 a week, would materially increase wages, by providing work for many who are now in enforced idleness, thus reducing competition for employment. This would make it possible for those workers who are underpaid to obtain advances, because the abundant supply of labour would be lessened, and thus new demands would be made for commodities, resulting in a large increase in production, cheapening of commodities, and increased aggregate profits.

The demand we, as workmen, now make is for

Leisure, not idleness.

Leisure to think, to learn, to acquire knowledge, to enjoy, to develop; in short, Leisure to Live.

The Demand Justified by Economics

Economic ignorance has in times past caused us to believe that our duty lay in the direction of producing much and consuming little; this is a fatal error. Those who consume least are the most ignorant, the most useless, and the most animal-like of all. A large consuming capacity on the part of every section of workers is fully justified by sound economics. The agricultural labourer, with 10s. a week, must vegetate like the plants - his low purchasing power does not admit of healthy, hearty social intercourse. At times he yearns for concerts, for theatres, for light-hearted joviality; would be delighted to be well-dressed, and have his wife and children well-dressed; would like even a fortnight's holiday to see some other part of the country than the few fields and farmyard he is familiar with; but, ah! He has no money, and he might as well wish himself lord of the manor as wish to ever gratify these simple and legitimate tastes.

It is quite true that, if he had money enough, and spent it on clothes, and furniture, and books, and concerts, and holiday-making, he would be helping others to get equally good conditions; but the farm labourer of England, poor wretch, is hemmed in, chained to a ten times accursed poverty, and he can neither help himself to good things, nor his fellow workers. We will say nothing of what he may do for the landlord at present.

An Example to Other Trades

Much the same is true of the men have worked in and about the coal mines. Fixed to the miners' village, with an occasional run to the nearest town, the pitman's family gets familiarised to the scenery of the pit bank, engine house, pulleys and frame, the throbbing of the winding engine, and, at night, to the burning of the waste-heap. The miner, like the agricultural labourer, is chained. But the miner is, at last, about to burst the chain asunder; he has learned the a value of sectional organisation, and now has actually federated most of these sectional unions into two large federations for the country, with a prospect of, ere long, all men in and about the pits being under one banner. 430,000 men already on their feet, and now demanding an eight hour day. Will they get it? Certainly. But how? There's the rub; and my object in writing this pamphlet is to contribute some little to the discussion of

How to Get the Eight Hour Day

rather than to point out its advantages; and being amongst those who have tried to think the question out, I am satisfied that the way to Freedom lies through the eight hour door, feeling assured that a daily or weekly limit of working hours is possible of application to all employees.

At the Trades Union Congress held at Liverpool last year, a resolution was carried in favour of obtaining an eight hour day by "Parliamentary enactment, " the lost amendment declaring, in decided terms, in favour of the eight hour day, but to relegate the question to

Parliament "would indefinitely delay this much needed reform." Subsequent events have shown that there is a great waste of energy going on by the "legalists" combating the "voluntary" advocates, and vice versa, in a manner that makes sport for the Philistines rather than enhancing the cause both sections have at heart, and we are now entitled to ask: Is there not

A Middle Course

that can be adopted, which will command at once the endorsement and support of both sections?

Briefly stated, the argument of

The Voluntary Men,

or those who favour the obtaining of a reduction of working hours by trade union effort only, not supplemented by legislative enactment, is as follows:- Parliament is hostile to labour's interests, is composed of men who do not understand, and have no desire to understand, labour's requirements, and cannot, therefore, effectually legislate for labour; besides, those sections of workers who have obtained reductions of working hours to the limit now asked for, and even below it, have obtained the reduction entirely by voluntary trade effort, which has developed in them a sturdiness of character superior to that of their fellows who clamour for legislative assistance.

The Legalists

point with scorn to the fact that only a very small section of miners have successfully reduced working hours; that many others have tried to do so by means of their unions, but have in the majority of cases failed; that some two millions only are enrolled in trade unions, out of an adult working population of nine millions; that a trade unionist is still a citizen and has the fullest right to make use of the legislative institution in labour's interests; that to refuse to make use of Parliament, is carrying out a policy calculated to drift into anarchism, and that it is foolish to attempt to make these great changes by negotiations between employers and workers, resulting in strikes and lockouts, when the same end can be achieved more quickly by law.

Such, in effect, are the arguments most commonly used on either side, but of course there are many others of a similar character. These sections are continually combating each other, and thus bitterness and strife are engendered which it were more dignified to avoid. Fortunately, there are those who recognise expediency as the deciding point in this matter, and who, whilst they uphold all that is sturdy, manly, and true, in the arguments of the voluntary men, are fully alive to the desirability, fitness, and economic soundness of voluntary effort being supplemented and clenched by legislative enactment.

That a middle course is required, the following returns of the voting of the members of the Amalgamated Engineers just to hand - April 1891 - will indicate.

The financial reserves of this one union amount, roundly, to a quarter of a million; their numerical strength is 69,064 members, 62,500 of whom are in the United Kingdom; among these the votes have just been taken, with the following results:-

	For	Against
For an eight hour day	8, 149	1,290
For a 48 hour week	8,007	1,118

By legal enactment	3,275	4,901
By trade union effort	6,546	1,251

It will be seen that the total number whose votes are recorded for and against an eight hour day or 48 hour week, is 18,674 out of 62,500 in the United Kingdom, or less than one-third of the actual members; that is due to the fact that only one-third of the members on the average, are present on any one night, but there is no reason to suppose that the proportions would be materially altered if every vote were recorded. Of those recorded 16,256 are favourable either to the eight hour day or 48 hour week, and only 2,408 against these proposals, or a majority in favour of nearly seven to one.

But when we come to the method of how to obtain it, opinions are much more divided, there being two to one in favour of trade union effort as against legal enactment.

Does not this show clearly that, so far as the engineers are typical of the other trades, neither by legal enactment nor by trade union effort are we likely to secure the reduced' hours, and therefore a middle course is absolutely necessary?

Five years ago the discussion of this question had scarcely assumed a definite shape. The position taken up by its advocates then was to declare generally in favour of an Eight Hours Bill for all trades, and this served the purpose of arresting attention, and enabling the eight hour men to demonstrate the fact that eight hours work as a maximum was possible and desirable.

We have now reached the stage when vague generalities must be replaced by definite particulars, calculated to command the respect and attention of those who are fully conversant with our complex industrial system.

The Workers' Demand

The working hours of most mechanics of this country are nominally fixed at nine a day, though two thirds of the workers work an average of eleven hours a day, and the remaining third thirteen hours. But this statement needs qualifying by a reminder of the startling and saddening fact that one-thirteenth of the working population is always in enforced idleness, which means that we have now of our adult working population some

700,000 Out of Work,

600,000 of whom are men, three-fifths having families depending upon them. A sufficient cause, indeed, to hasten on the immediate application, wherever possible, of a reduction of normal working hours.

To tabulate

The Various Methods

now before the country for reducing working hours, they are as follows:-

1st. Those who demand an Eight Hour Bill to apply to all trades and industries throughout the country, but are willing that a start should be made in all Government establishments, followed up by eight hours for railway men and miners.

2nd. Those who demand that it shall be left entirely for the workers to obtain it through their trade unions and labour organisations without any legislative assistance whatsoever.

3rd. Those who contend that the demand for an eight hour day, or 48 hours a week, shall be first made by the majority of any trade, who shall have the right to make known to the Secretary of State their desire for working hours being fixed by law, and the Secretary of State to be empowered to give effect to their wishes. This is legislative enactment by trade option.

4th. Those that contend that the least objectionable, most practicable, and, therefore, most expeditious method of obtaining reduced hours is, that Parliament shall pass an Act empowering local authorities to administer the same as follows: That when three-fifths of the adult workers in any trade in the district over which the local authority has jurisdiction, request that their working hours be fixed at a maximum of eight hours per shift, or 48 hours in one week, the local authority, being satisfied that the demand is rightly made, shall notify the employers in that district that in three months from the date of the application having been made, the law will be enforced, under a monetary penalty for every person employed contrary to the provisions of the Act.

This is local trade option, the initiative in every case being taken by the workers engaged in the trade or calling, no action being taken by the authorities until requested so to do by three-fifths of the adult workers engaged in the trade.

Local Trade Option

method that commends itself to me, for the following reasons:-

(a) It is free from the objections lodged against No. 1 - the Bill of universal application which would force the eight hour limit upon those who had not asked for it, and would not make allowance for those trades where the difficulties of applying the limit are very great, and where in the opinion of the majority of workers and employers at present engaged in these

The Workers' Demand

trades, the limit, if applied suddenly, would prove disastrous. That there are such trades is well known; and, although the Universal Bill men may wish to treat them with impunity, that does not settle the matter, nor can it be said to be statesmanship of a very valuable kind, that would ruthlessly and needlessly ride rough-shod over the desires of an important minority of citizens.

(b) It is free from the objection lodged against No. 2 - the narrow trade union method - as it fully recognizes the wisdom and desirability of supplementing trade union effort by legislation. It upholds, every solid contention that is advanced by the old trade union or voluntary effort section, by insisting that the demand shall be made by the workers themselves in each trade or calling, and that they must show their desire for the limiting of working hours by a three-fifths majority, which throws the educational and organising work on to the shoulders of the trade unionists, who, by the local trade option method, will not be asking the State to do for them that which they might do for themselves; but will simply be working by what they conceive to be the better of several methods open to them.

(c) It is free from an objection very rightly lodged against No. 3 - trade option (without local) method - which is that if the workers in any trade - say engineering - in London are thoroughly educated up to the eight hour demand, and manifest much interest and keen anxiety to get the same as the result of years of agitation and organisation in their ranks, and if a similar number of men in other parts of the country, say Glasgow, where organisation is less complete, and the desire for shorter hours is less marked, that the London men who have organised and educated themselves, must wait years for the beneficial change, because in other districts there is little or no interest in the subject. This cannot be looked upon with satisfaction, nor is it in accordance with common sense. Trade option coupled with local option carries with it no such disadvantage, but on the other hand, it is in complete accord with the independent spirit exhibited by the more enlightened and sturdy of British workmen, who are alive to the necessity of a Governmental controlling hand, but who also insist upon the fullest possible recognition of local autonomy consistent with harmonious working throughout the country.

This voluntary effort method, supplemented by legislation, should command the support of the vast majority of those who have been advocating the reduction of working hours, either as trade unionists or "legalists," as practically all the voluntary men believe in the State machine, even to the extent of sending their own workmates to manage it - as in the case of the Northumberland and Durham miners, whilst the "legalists," or at least those who have become conspicuous, are members of one or other of the trade organisations.

A Peculiar Feature

in the mental make-up of not a few of the determined "legalists" of to-day is the fact that only three or four years ago they were opponents both of an eight hour working day and of trades unionism. Something more far-reaching than an eight hour day was wanted, and even should the workers, in their ignorance, condescend to accept an eight hour day, it would block the solution of the "social problem." The eight hour men persisted, with the result that it's former opponents on advanced lines have proved their capacity to learn by becoming advocates of the same themselves, and a revival took place eventually in the ranks of the trade unions; but the advanced men had already to their satisfaction sealed the doom of unionism. There might be a "flutter," said these critics, but as to trade unions ever being worth a serious thought as a means for solving industrial questions, was not admitted. However, the unions grew, old and new alike, and the one million-and-a-quarter of members of two years ago have increased to the two millions of to-day, and, behold! among them are to be found the cynics of eighteen months ago, and these gentlemen are not only members, but it is to be feared, in some instances, are mischievous members, by encouraging a policy that teaches, in effect, that the unions are valuable only in proportion as they are made vote-controlling institutions.

Value of a Trade Union.

Now, there can be no objection to a trade organisation encouraging its members to take a lively interest in municipal and parliamentary questions that affect the .cause of labour; on the contrary, it should be an important item in the programme of every union; but the union itself, as an institution, is of the highest value to the State. Those who imagine that unions are simply wage-regulating machines, and serviceable only as such, make a serious mistake. To hundreds of thousands of workmen in Great Britain they are far and away the most valuable of all institutions for gathering knowledge, for imparting information, for discussions of detail matters in connection with labour that require constant attention, and upon which the very existence of our industrial well-being depends, and it is in this capacity that the unions are eminently capable of rendering valuable assistance, yes, positive guidance to their own members, and outsiders, as to the changes that may with advantages be made in our complex industry system. It is, therefore, pre-eminently a question for them to decide as to how far we may with advantage make changes in curtailing working hours. Of course, care must be taken that the opinions of officials are not taken as the opinions of the members, but we may safely leave members to deal with their officials, as although for a time a reactionary policy may be endorsed by officialdom, contrary to the desire of rank and file, the officials that would be unwise enough to resist progress will be superseded by others more sympathetic with the times.

The Proposed Plan Clearly Defined

To again state that which is proposed as the local trade option method. It is,

(a) That an act be passed fixing the maximum working hours at eight a day, or eight and a half for five days, and five and a half for the sixth (or made up in such other method as may be agreed upon), but not to exceed 48 hours a week, *overtime to be a punishable offence, both for employer and worker*, except in cases of special emergency, such as "breakdowns, &c.," or in the case of agricultural labourers, when special provision would be made for harvest-time.

(b) That the administration of this Act shall be left with the County Council, Town Council, Local Board, or such other local authority as shall be clearly specified by the Act.

(c) That it shall be left with the adult workers of either sex, engaged in any trade or calling, to obtain the clearly expressed opinion of those engaged in the trade as to whether or not they wish for the Act to be applied to them, and that in the event of three-fifths being in favour of the same, their request be sent to the local authority responsible for the administration of the Act, which, being satisfied that the request is genuine shall immediately notify the employers in the district that the provision of the Act will be put in force at a date of three months from the time application was made to them by the workers.

Advantages of the Scheme.

The special advantages this method secures are:-

(a) It affords better opportunity than any of the other methods to each section to make as much or as little use of law as they think desirable.

(b) It admits of the thorough carrying out of the principle of local autonomy, and leaves those who know most about each trade to be the judges as to when and how the working hours shall be fixed.

(c) It affords the advantages of legislation to those who appreciate the same, and admits of the industrial change taking place gradually, beginning immediately with those trades where the stated majority is favourable, and thus deprives the opponents of the shorter working day of one of their principal arguments, as to the dislocation brought about by a sudden jump all round.

Objections to the Scheme.

In opposition to the trade option method with local application, it is contended that we shall intensify the differences that already exist between different localities rather than remove them by such a scheme, and engineers have asked, "How can we have Leeds and Bradford dealt with under this proposal where the class of trade is the same, when, to reduce working hours at Leeds, and not at Bradford, or vice versa, would certainly create discord of a serious nature?"

This same argument could be used with equal force by every trade that is termed national, and the reply is, that the trade unions in which, at least, important sections of the men are enrolled - and which will, undoubtedly, take the initiative in these matters - would advise the members as to when and where the application should be made, and as regards the engineers, there would be little difficulty in classifying their trade, and the districts in which it is carried on.

Thus, the Eastern Counties are mainly devoted to the production of agricultural engines and machinery, whilst the Tyne, Wear, Tees, Hartlepools and Clyde are specially devoted to marine engineering and shipbuilding; Lancashire and Yorkshire are largely at work on cotton and woollen machinery; again, Crewe, Swindon, Doncaster, and other railway centres are engaged on locomotives; Birmingham, Manchester, and Sheffield employ many thousands on tools and war implements; each class of trade is practically complete within itself, and the unit of area as regards the union's efforts should be the entire district, or districts, in which a particular class of trade is carried on.

Thus, with the makers of machinery for farming, it would be necessary to deal with the towns of Lincoln, Ipswich, Grantham, Colchester, Gainsboro', and other places where this trade exists. The union could supervise operations, and make a simultaneous demand in each of these centres.

For the shipbuilding centres the same could be adopted, and thus uniformity of action secured wherever the same class of trade prevailed. So that instead of being more difficult of application, the local option clause would give the necessary elasticity, admitting of adjustments being made far easier than by any other method yet proposed.

It is quite evident that

Trade Cannot be Localised,

and on behalf of the Scotch jute mills it has been contended that we cannot pit town against town; but it has been shown in the example given, by classifying the engineering trade, that we could effectively meet the requirements of that trade. So with the jute mills of Forfarshire, viz., Dundee, Forfar, Arbroath, Kirriemuir, Brechin, and Montrose, simultaneous action could be taken. Already many of these workers are organised, and their unions are gaining in strength every week, and by means of their union the difficulties alluded to could be overcome.

At the Congress last year no men were more opposed to legal enactment than the cotton-spinners and weavers of Lancashire and Yorkshire, one of their contentions being that the competition of India is so keen that they ought to be allowed to decide for themselves when and how they shall obtain reduced hours. The argument is a sound one. Why should they not? Let those trades who are ready for the change set the pace, and the cotton and woollen workers will soon follow on, and all the quicker by having freedom to adopt their own time and method.

The boot and shoe trade could be similarly arranged for by means of the unions. One class of work is carried on at Bristol, another at Northampton, and a mixed trade in London; but the unions are quite capable of classifying the trades and the districts.

The tailoring could be covered in the same way, and so on with every trade throughout the country.

Take the Miners' Case.

In Durham and Northumberland the coal hewers and stonemen - about 60 per cent of those engaged in and about the mines - work seven hours from bank to bank, but the remainder of the workmen and boys work eleven hours, that is the pit begins at six in the morning, and works right on till five at night, and a large proportion of the 40 per cent of men who commence and finish at these hours, have no break for meals the whole day. Thus it is not true that short hours cover the whole of those at work in the Northumberland and Durham coalfields. But the decision of the men alluded to, so far as it has been given expression to at Trades Congresses, is decidedly against legislative action. I have mixed with these miners a good deal, and am of opinion that the 40 per cent who work at least 10 and-a-half hours a day would be very glad indeed to have their hours reduced by legislation or otherwise, and this belief exists with the members of the Miners' Federation of Great Britain, whose working hours vary from eight to eleven a day. This federation is distinctly favourable to legislative action, but so far it has been unable to obtain it. An Act is asked for forbidding more than eight hours work from bank to bank, and this is opposed by the workmen M.P.'s of Durham and Northumberland, as well as by the mine owners and other capitalists. Would it not be well for the members to favour the local option method, and thus secure at once the co-operation of Durham and Northumberland, who would undoubtedly vote with the Federation men to get legislation for themselves, providing it did not cover the Northumberland and Durham men, who do not want it? How was the last 10 per cent advance obtained by this great Federation? By the Bristol Miners' Association as part of the Federation, and representing fourteen collieries in Gloucester and Somerset, deciding in favour of five per cent down and the other five in three months. That forced the pace, and right from Monmouthshire to Yorkshire the advance was conceded in a week; the employers being forced to give it because one locality led the way. If we had local option in the matter of fixing hours legislatively, it is very probable that similar results would follow and if Durham and Northumberland really prefer to have nothing to do with legislation in this matter of working hours, let them have their way. Should those who now have the shorter working day be unable to retain it without legislative enactment, they may be relied upon to change their opinions rather than their hours of work, and it is a pity to find men like Mr. Pickard, on the one side, and Mr. Burt, on the other, continually endeavouring to convert each other when by different tactics both might have their way, and thus have energy to devote to other purposes. Nothing can please the enemies of labour better than to find labour leaders opposed to each other, and it behoves us all to adopt that course best calculated to leave the fullest freedom for all to enjoy their own opinion, when this can be done consistently with labour's interests receiving due attention.

The Dock and Riverside Workers.

In connection with the various ports of Great Britain and Ireland, we have some 200,000 men employed about 70,000 of whom are engaged in the Port of London. There is probably no other class of men in the country whose occupation is so precarious. A small proportion have, of course, regular employment at regular wages, but, as a class, the stevedores, coal porters, riggers, dockers and lightermen, are subject to more disappointments than any other body of workers in the country. Many thousands who have followed up dock work all their lives never know what they will be able to earn during the week. A man will set out for work on a Monday morning, and after spending four or five hours holding himself ready for work, learns there is none that day; this is oftentimes repeated the whole week through, and in slack times it runs on for months, when there is not a stroke to be obtained; and yet while this is going on, in the same port, hundreds of men will be working overtime, commonly making 80 or more hours a week, and the men who have been hanging on, when they get a start, are frequently called upon to work most excessive hours for a short time, and being hard up they always try to do it. We want a maximum fixing, beyond which no man shall be allowed to work, both in his own interest and that of his fellows. It is a shameful thing that in London there should be, as there always is, men at the docks and wharves working 60 to 80 hours a week, and others not working at all. It would be difficult to fix a daily limit at such work, but it would not be difficult to fix a weekly limit, and if we had an Act of Parliament which could be applied by the local authorities, we could very soon do much towards steadying the employment of thousands of men whose lives are now half wasted by lack of system that prevails in this matter of working hours.

Confining our attention to London, it might be added that, in addition to the regulation of hours by fixing a weekly maximum, it is in the highest degree necessary that the trade of this, the first port in the world, should not be left to the tender mercies of competing dock companies and wharf proprietors, with conflicting interests, operating disastrously to the labourers by the want of anything approaching uniformity. But it is high time the London County Council seriously considered the practicability of taking entire control of the dock and wharves, and conducting the trade of the same interests of the community, and employing workers, as far as possible, on a uniform plan, respecting their employees as citizens of no mean city., regulating the number of men to meet the exigencies of season trades, with as little hardship to the labourer as possible, instead of the present plan of dispensing immediately with the services of every man possible one month, and going bull-rush at it the next.

The Port of London for the People of London

must be pressed on by every workman who realises how much might be done to steady the labourer's occupation, if the port were controlled by one competent authority instead of by 150 authorities, as at present.

To again refer to the Trades Congress of last year, held at Liverpool, it was regretted by many that such unanimity should prevail as regards the desirability of an eight hour day, or 48 hours a week, and that such strong differences of opinion should exist respecting the method to be adopted to bring this about.

This year's Congress is to be held in Newcastle-upon-Tyne, a city where the workers are well organised, and in the heart of the district where the "voluntary effort" men and "legislative enactment advocates" alike are very earnest and decided in defending their respective views.

Are we again to witness similar division to that of last year? It will be a shame and a disgrace to us all if this is allowed. In order to test the feeling of a number of trade unionists, the following was submitted to and accepted by them, as a resolution containing the idea

The Eight Hour Day

I have tried to convey, and I simply give it here so that members of trade societies may raise the question in their branches, and thus bring the subject before their members:

> "That this Congress is of opinion that the most expeditious and practical method of securing an eight hour working day, or 48 hour week, is by trade union initiative supplemented by legislative enactment, locally applied, whenever and wherever three-fifths of the adult workers in any trade or calling desire the same, and we hereby instruct the Parliamentary Committee to frame and introduce a Bill on trade option lines (for local administration) at their earliest opportunity, and we call upon all trade unionists and friends of labour to press the same forward by every means in their power. "

This might secure unanimity of action, which would very soon result in our securing the passing of the Bill. It is argued by some that it would be as difficult to get such a Bill passed as to get a universal eight hours Bill for immediate application. This I do not believe for two reasons: first, because the local option method admits of a gradual change to suit the requirements of the localities, which would thereby remove much opposition now shown to a universal Bill; and second, because by forcing it on more, we should get the support instead of the opposition of those who object to legislation in their own trade, but who respect the wishes of those engaged in other trades differently circumstanced.

But I advocate this method for one other important reason, and that is, that local autonomy in these matters is right in principle, and beneficial in practice, whereas to encourage the notion that Parliament is an all-wise institution, and capable of dealing with the details of our complex industrial system is wrong in principle, and bad in practice; but we need not necessarily run to the other extreme, and refuse to make use of Parliament for those purposes that it can serve as no other institution can, by Its power to ratify, enforce, and, where necessary, to unify the expressed desire of the majority.

The Land Question

According to the official statistics, we import food stuffs into this country to the value of £ 140,000,000 a year, and it appears to be generally thought that the land of this country is incapable of supplying us with these food stuffs. We have heard so much about farmers being unable to cultivate at a profit that many have become impressed with the notion that it is really all over with this country from a food- producing standpoint.

And yet, upon investigation, one finds that one-fourth of the land of the United Kingdom is lying idle, producing nothing, while on those portions properly cultivated as a large a crop can be obtained as from any land in the world.

The system of large farms in this country has proved a failure. Rent is a first charge upon the landlord's rent, or the crops would be the landlords. In bad years, this pressure of landlordism upon the farmers has been so severe that, in order to have the cash for the rent, they have been compelled to retrench somewhere, and, although to discharge the men was certain to ruin the farmer ultimately, they have, year by year, discharged the farm labourers, until the land is now absolutely labour starved; four men only are employed where at least six are required if good results are to be obtained. Three quarters of wheat per acre only are produced on land which, with proper cultivation, will yield six to seven quarters. The labourers being thus discharged, have been compelled to leave the villages and make for the towns, and in this way at least

200,000 Farm Labourers

have been driven from the villages, by this process of retrenchment on the part of the farmers to meet the £60,000,000 a year demanded from them by the landlords. Many have thought that it is because machinery has been introduced on the land that these farm labourers have made to the towns; that is a minor cause. Machinery is not largely used on land in this country. The difficulty has been brought about by the private ownership of land, and the owners pressing the cultivators for rent; driving them into a corner, from which they have been, in many cases, unable to extricate themselves.

In consequence, it is now difficult to let large farms, and a return will certainly be made to the small farm system again. But more important still is the fact that the labourer is now claiming the right to cultivate land on his own account. He sees that if he can get an acre or acre-and-a-half he can easily cultivate this in his broken time, and that it will be worth 4s 6d or 5s a week to him each acre he cultivates. But his difficulty is to get it. To be of service it must be within a mile of his cottage, as otherwise he cannot reach it to put in his odd time. It must also be obtainable at a fair rent - by fair here is meant fair when compared with that the farmers pay for land of a similar quality. Instances can be given where the farmers pay 30s per acre and for exactly the same quality the labourer is charged 80s per acre.

The Allotment Act

of 1887 is an incomplete and unworkable affair, nevertheless it is the recognition of a vital principle, viz., that under it the labourers have the right to make application to the rural sanitary authority for any piece of land that may suit their purpose for allotments, and the Act empowers the rural sanitary authority to purchase this land and let the same to the labourers. We have here the municipalisation of the land actually in process. Unfortunately, landowners often refuse to let, and litigation ensues, and the cost of the land is run excessively high by the legal costs and by an additional 10 per cent, above value, which the Act empowers the owner to charge, so that so far very few allotments have been obtained under the Act, but it has caused many farmers and owners to come to terms by a mutual arrangement with the labourers, and many hundreds of allotments are now being cultivated by labourers in their odd and broken time.

And here comes the value of the eight hours to these farm-labourers. There is no reason why the proposed 48 hours a week should not apply to them. They work now about 11 hours a day (Saturday included); but if they organize as they are now doing, they will, with the aid of their fellow trade unionists in the towns, be able to obtain the Saturday half-holiday and a weekly maximum of 48 hours. The daily limit could not rigidly be applied, and the necessary elasticity would have to be arranged for to provide for harvesting, but this is only some five or six weeks in the year.

When, by means of trade unionism, they are able to make a firm stand, and demand, through the proper channels, the establishing of parish councils - which will simply be an extension of the Local Government Act - and obtain the reduced working hours, then they will be able, by means of their parish council, to obtain what land is necessary, conveniently situated, on fair terms, for allotments, and they will be able to supply the towns with the necessary food stuffs, including fruit, eggs, and dairy produce; they will be able to live in comparative comfort themselves, as they will no longer be wholly dependent upon farmer or squire.

A few years successful cultivation of an allotment will enable a man to go in for small holding of from ten to thirty acres upon which he will be well able to keep his family, and of course give up working for the farmer, and thus again will England become a food-producing country of the first order and the countrymen supplying the food requirements of the towns will, in turn, make large demands for clothing and furniture, &c., for themselves. There are in the United Kingdom at least 15,000,000 acres of uncultivated land, all capable of profitable cultivation, according to the evidence given before the Royal Commission on Agriculture; this must be brought under cultivation, and the land now labour starved be properly worked, and by these means employment will be found in abundance for a peasantry four times as numerous as that we now have, and the people of the British Isles will be able to obtain butter without fetching it from Denmark. Whilst I lay especial stress upon the reduction of working hours as set forth in this pamphlet, I would guard readers against supposing that reduced working hours alone will rid our towns of poverty, and, therefore, we must go deeper still. The land question, as it affects both town and country, intimately affects our every day life, and must receive adequate attention. Till this is done the labour problem can never be solved, and our brightest hopes now are raised by the fact that at last townsmen and countrymen are beginning to see that their interests are identical, that they must work together for a common object, that villagers can help townsmen and vice versa, and that if we refuse to be pitted against each other, as we have been in the past, that then there are grounds for believing the day of our deliverance from poverty is at hand, and that peace and plenty will yet be ours.

In conclusion, I would urge upon all, but especially upon trade unionists, to be sensibly jealous of wasting their energy - the work of life is difficult enough without our combating each other. Let us not forget that ours is the cause of **BROTHERHOOD**, and that our actions must fit with our phrases. We are striving to realise the ideal that Thomas Carlyle yearned for, that John Ruskin has preached and worked for, and which the poet Burns bids us pray for.

For further reading

Dona Torr. Tom Mann Memoirs. Publisher: Lawrence and Wishart

Allen Hutt. British Trade Unionism. Publisher: Lawrence and Wishart

James B Jeffreys. The Story of the Engineers. Publisher: Lawrence and Wishart

Terry McCarthy. Dock Strike 1889. Publisher: Weidenfeld and Nicolson

Walter Southgate

Socialist

Walter Southgate was the quintessential rank-and-file activist born in East London in 1890 of working-class parents.

Walter enjoyed the comforts of a typical east London two-up, two-down cottage. He excelled at school and should have gone into further education, but the financial situation at home ensured that he left school at 14.

Although Walter's parents had no funds for him to be indentured into one the arts and crafts trades, he found employment as a junior clerk in a solicitor's office and soon mastered the intricacies of the legal profession, especially trade union and Labour law. When his employer asked if he wanted to be a solicitor, in typical Southgate fashion he answered 'both you and I know I haven't the money and I come from the wrong class'.

He used his legal skills when he took up employment with the National Union of Clark's - he was their delegate to Hackney Trades Council. Walter was then a member of Hyman's Marxist Social Democratic Federation. Through his Trades Council, he was a delegate to the Labour Representation Committee.

Walter Southgate was a lover of the outdoors and was instrumental in forming the Hackney branch of the Clarion Cycle Club. Both his skills as a graphic artist and writer were used by the Clarion movement. Walter was the author and compiler of the Clarion yearbook and designed leaflets, posters and other art propaganda for the movement until the First World War.

Walter, like many Socialists, saw the First World War as an imperialist war and refused to fight. Famously, when the magistrate from the tribunal cross-examined Walter on why he wouldn't fight, asking 'didn't he want to defend his home?' Walter answered that 'the Kaiser must be really hard-up if he wants my house!' Walter than went on the trot, working where he could in the country, keeping his head down throughout the war years.

In 1920 became clerk to the Sheet Metal Workers Union a post which he held until 1943.

Walter continued to be an active Socialist, writing many articles for the socialist press and acting as secretary to his Trades Council and trade union branch as well as being an active member of the Labour Party and he gave free advice to the local community. In 1943 Walter took up the post of rehousing and rest centre officer for those who had been blitzed.

Walter understood the value of working class memorabilia and history and in the 1960s he teamed up with Henry Fry and the Trade Union, Labour, Co-operative History Society whose aim was to set-up a Labour History Museum to preserve the people's history and to propagate socialism. Walter donated his unique archive to this cause and his dream was realised when in 1975 the Labour History Museum in Limehouse, London was opened by the then Prime Minister Harold Wilson. Walter saw the museum grow from one room in the old Limehouse Town Hall to the entire building.

Walter had a wicked sense of humour. This was demonstrated when Walter was awarded the Golden Badge of Merit for services to the Labour Party by the then Prime Minister James Callahan: Walter enquired if the warrant was still out for him!.

For his full story, read 'That's the Way it was, a working class autobiography 1890-1950', edited by Terry Philpot and published by New Clarion Press.

T McCarthy, Walter Southgate Trust.

www.ingramcontent.com/pod-product-compliance
Ingram Content Group UK Ltd.
Pitfield, Milton Keynes, MK11 3LW, UK
UKHW041433180426
11947UKWH00007B/421